The Pedlar's Caps

Retold by Annette Smith

Illustrated by Naomi C Lewis

NELSON PRICE MILBURN

"Caps for sale! Caps for sale!"
called the young pedlar
as he walked through the town.

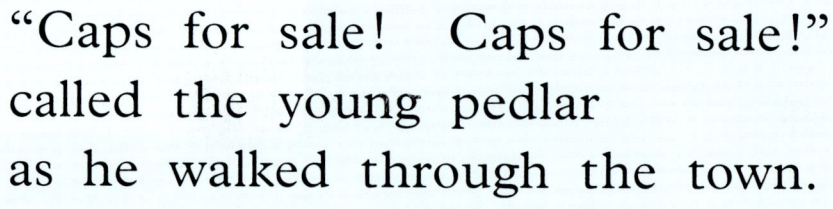

He was different from other pedlars
because he didn't have a cart,
or a pack, or even a tray.
He carried his caps
in a pile on top of his head.

He had to walk very carefully.

The caps were always piled up
in the same order.
First, the young pedlar wore
his own embroidered cap.
On top of this sat
a pile of yellow caps,
then some blue caps,
some purple caps
and, right at the top,
all the bright red caps.

People often came hurrying
out of their houses
just to watch him go by.

But today, as the pedlar walked
along the street calling,
"Caps for sale! Caps for sale!"
no one came out.

So he decided
to leave the town
and walk out into the country.
After a while,
he began to feel tired.
He sat down
in the shade of a tree
with the pile of caps
still on his head.

The day was very hot,
and he was soon fast asleep.

When the young pedlar woke up,
he put his hand up to his head
to feel his pile of caps.
The caps were gone!
His embroidered cap
was the only one left.

He looked in front of him.
He looked behind him.
He looked all around him.

No caps! Where were they?
Where **had** they gone?

The young pedlar heard something rustle high in the tree.
He looked up, and he saw flashes of yellow and blue and purple and red.

There, sitting in the branches,
was a big troop of monkeys,
and every monkey
was wearing a cap!

"Hey!" called the young pedlar.
"Give me back my caps!"

The monkeys chattered back at him.

He shook his stick at the monkeys,
and the monkeys shook
the branches of the tree.

The young pedlar was now very angry.
He shook his fist at the monkeys,
and the monkeys shook their fists
back at him.

He was so angry
that he took his own cap
off his head
and threw it to the ground.

Then all the monkeys
took off their caps
and threw **them**
to the ground, too!

The pedlar started to laugh.
He piled all the caps
onto his head
very quickly indeed,
and walked back
down the road.
He was still laughing
when he got to the town.
"Caps for sale! Caps for sale!"
he called.